Judo

for

Juniors

Nicolas Soames

LEOPARD

This edition published in 1997 by Leopard Books,
a division of Random House UK Limited
20 Vauxhall Bridge Road,
London SW1V 2SA

First published in 1991 by Stanley Paul.

ISBN 0 7529 0438 8

Typeset in Rockwell and Helvetica by SX Composing Ltd,
Rayleigh, Essex

Contents

	Acknowledgements	4
	Foreword by Neil Adams	5
1	How judo began	6
2	The dojo and its etiquette	10
3	The kit	14
4	The grades	16
5	Warming-up and breakfalls	19
6	The throws	26
7	Combinations and counters	44
8	Ground work	54
9	Practice	70
10	Rules and scoring	75
11	Competition	79
12	Kata	87
13	Japan and the Japanese	94

Acknowledgements

My thanks go to David Finch, the tireless and patient judo photographer whose work both at demonstration sessions and competitions dominate the book; to Eddie Ferrie, who took the photos in Japan; to Alan Rickard, for Jigoro Kano's statue outside the Kodokan; to Tim Green for his photos of Ian Freeman in competition; and to John Gichigi for his expert printing.

The bulk of the demonstration shots were taken at the Camberley Judo Club, under the direction of its chief instructor, Mark Earle. Erica Bowley, Debbie Allan, Ian Freeman and Danny Kingston were the able demonstrators. The cover shot was taken at the Neil Adams Club, Coventry, just before a hard but enjoyable practice.

Additional techniques were demonstrated by Ben Soames and Ben Andersen at The Budokwai, London. And the kata was performed by Andrew and Lisa Paveley (St Albans Judo Club) at the Tokei Club in London.

Hiroko Mori kindly drew the kanji, hiragana and katakana, and checked the Japanese.

My thanks to all concerned – they reflect the skill and enthusiasm in all areas of judo that exists among the up-and-coming generation of judo players in this country.

Foreword

1

● Judo is a very special sport – and that's not just because it is the sport which took over my life.

For a start, it is great fun. There are few things more satisfying than catching your partner with a big throw like seoi-nage or tai-otoshi which takes him right up into the air and then flat down to the mat. Or, after a short tussle on the ground, manoeuvering your partner into a hold and keeping him there, no matter how hard he struggles.

These are the most dramatic bits of judo. But what makes them so satisfying is that they haven't happened through sheer luck – but because of all the training that has gone before. Judo is not just about fighting, it is about developing skills which will work whichever club you go to.

I was lucky because my father was a black belt and taught me my basic judo. He insisted that I didn't just fight to score points, but tried to develop really good technique. He even stopped me entering too many competitions when I was young because he thought it wouldn't be good for my judo in the long run – and circumstances proved him right.

When I was a junior, I threw most of my opponents in competition with morote-seoi-nage. But when I was around 15 and got my black belt, my opponents learned how to stop it and I started to get injured. My father told me to switch to tai-otoshi. At first it didn't work, and I would slip in a morote-seoi-nage when I thought my father wasn't watching. But little by little the tai-otoshi began to work. Eventually it became one of my strongest techniques – my very last throw in international competition (in the Seoul Olympics) was tai-otoshi. I scored ippon.

So developing good technique is very important. At my judo club in Coventry, all my young students spend as much time practising throws and ground work as they spend on randori, fitness or weight training. Some of the best sessions are technique-only practices!

The emphasis in this book is on good technique from the very start. That also means good breakfalls and good etiquette – all of which help to prevent injuries and make judo more enjoyable.

I practised regularly with Nicolas Soames at my club in London, The Budokwai and he visited me when I taught in France and Japan and other countries. He helped me write my first book, and started a special series, Judo Masterclass, written by champions from across the world. So he understands judo well.

And he doesn't just write about it. Whenever he travels abroad for his work as a journalist, he packs his judogi, and visits the local club – he has done judo in almost as many countries as I have.

But he has also taught in schools and clubs and he feels as strongly as I do that good technique from the beginning is very important.

The message from both of us is: Enjoy your judo. Develop good technique – and whether you want to stay in your club or whether you dream of being a world champion, you have a sport for life.

NEIL ADAMS
6th Dan

CHAPTER ONE

How judo began

● As a boy, Jigoro Kano was quite small for his age. He lived in Japan, where people are not very big – except for the occasional sumo wrestler – but Jigoro felt particularly small and weak. He went to school in Tokyo, the busy capital of Japan, and the bigger boys bullied him. This was partly because of his size and partly because he came from the country and wasn't accustomed to life in a fast city.

There are bullies in every country in the world, and they always look for easy targets – and at first Jigoro was no different.

He was born in 1860 in Mikage, a village in Setsu province near the modern city of Kobe on the main Japanese island of Honshu. It was a time when Japan

was still very traditional. There were no trains or machines, and everyone wore traditional dress – the kimono. The samurai, the Japanese warriors, still walked around the streets with two swords tucked into their belt – the matching pair were called dai-sho.

But as Jigoro grew up, Japan was changing. Sailing ships and steam ships from Europe and America were crossing the oceans to trade, and Japan was just starting to learn about the Western ideas and Western society. Jigoro's father watched his son do well in his early years at school and realised that he was quick and bright at his lessons. "Jigoro will have a better chance in life if we leave the country and move to the capital," thought Mr Kano. "It won't be easy, but he will get a wider education, and will have more opportunities when he finishes school and university and starts work."

So when Jigoro was 11, the Kano family decided to leave Mikage and travel to Tokyo, which was not an easy thing to do at the time. However, it proved the right thing because although Tokyo was very strange after the quiet country life, Jigoro showed that he was intelligent and hard-working: he always produced good marks at secondary school. But that didn't help him against the bullies. When he went to school in the morning, and when he returned home at night, he was pushed around and sometimes knocked to the ground. He didn't like complaining to his father and wanted to sort it out himself. So he turned to the old Japanese art of unarmed self-defence, ju-jitsu ("the soft art").

No one really knows when ju-jitsu started. The original ideas had probably come many centuries ago from China, where it was developed by Buddhist monks who wanted to protect themselves and others without swords or spears. These techniques were learned and adopted by the Japanese samurai for use if they were disarmed in battle. All warriors were taught basic techniques to use if they were disarmed or dropped their weapons, and they proved very effective.

Many different kinds of ju-jitsu schools developed. They taught all kinds of special tricks. These included throwing opponents into the air and hard down to the ground; or strangling them unconscious; or holding them tightly on the ground so that they couldn't escape; or dislocating limbs, which was very painful. They also taught punches and kicks.

Jigoro knew that here he could learn to defend himself. Every day after school – before he did his homework – he would go to the ju-jitsu school to learn the techniques and practise them.

He worked diligently at his ju-jitsu and didn't seem to mind the many knocks he got. It was a hard training – the older students in the ju-jitsu school didn't believe in going easy, even though Jigoro was just beginning and he was small. He was always covered with bruises, but he still kept on training. He used a special cream which smelt rather bad but cleared up the bruises quickly so that he could continue training. Soon the bullies learned to leave him alone.

Even though he had achieved his object, Kano continued to go to ju-jitsu every evening. While at university, Kano visited many different ju-jitsu schools, trying to pick up as many techniques as he could so that he was always able to handle his opponents, no matter how big or fast they were.

In one dojo (the Japanese word for "training hall") was a man called Fukushima who was much taller and heavier than Kano, and, try as he might, Jigoro couldn't sweep him off his feet. For weeks he tried different techniques without success. He tried everything he knew, but Fukushima stopped every attack and stayed on his feet.

So Jigoro went back to the old ju-jitsu books containing information which had been kept secret from most people. In one of those dusty scrolls he found a technique called "kata-guruma" (shoulder wheel) which he thought would work against Fukushima. He practised it in his own dojo in secret, and then visited the man to try it out. It worked perfectly – his oppo-

3

Above: The Japanese samurai in battle

Left: Professor Jigoro Kano, the originator of judo

nent was caught totally by surprise, lifted high into the air despite his weight, and thrown flat on his back.

Jigoro worked so hard at ju-jitsu that he wore out his thick jacket. It can still be seen in Tokyo – it is in tatters.

When Jigoro was 23, he decided to start his own school of ju-jitsu. Many of the ju-jitsu schools that existed in Japan at the time were not very good and were also very old-fashioned. The training was very rough and there were many injuries. Jigoro knew how exciting ju-jitsu could be, and interesting too. But he wanted to start a kind of ju-jitsu where young people could train without getting serious injuries.

One of his basic ideas, for example, was that everyone should learn to fall properly. When he started ju-jitsu, beginners were just thrown across a room and landed with a painful thump. But Jigoro wanted to teach his beginners to fall comfortably. He also wanted to introduce better behaviour.

"I want my pupils to be polite to each other, to take care with beginners and those who are not very experienced; and also to be polite to every one they meet," he said.

So, in 1882, Jigoro opened his own dojo. It was a small room, with just eight traditional straw mats, in a part of Eishoji, a Buddhist temple in Tokyo. He was quite young to be a teacher, but on the very first day he had seven students, and each week more would join. He called his school Kodokan Judo. Although he didn't know it then, from that small room of eight mats was to grow an international movement, with judo clubs in almost every country in the world.

Although he was still young, he made some strict rules. One of the most famous was that it was forbidden for any of his students to use judo outside the dojo. Some students of the old ju-jitsu schools had been bullies themselves, and ju-jitsu didn't have a very good reputation. Jigoro wanted to change this. He said that his judo students had to run away if they were challenged, rather than give judo a bad reputation by getting involved in a fight in the street.

One strong student was attacked by 12 toughs from a rival school. He did exactly what Kano told him to do – he ran away. By mistake, he ran into a cul-de-sac, a dead-end street. He had to turn and face his attackers, some of whom were armed with sticks and even a sword. But he dispatched them one after another, until the remainder took flight. The police arrived on the scene and questioned the student, because some of the men were badly injured. But they let him go when they realised he was acting in self-defence. However, Jigoro still banned him from the Kodokan dojo for six months, because he had broken the rule!

There were also formal challenges from other ju-jitsu schools, but Kodokan Judo won most of the matches.

One of the most famous was the encounter between Shiro Saigo from Kano's Kodokan Judo and Entaro Kochi from the rival Tozuka Ryu. The event took place at the Police Headquarters in Tokyo in 1887 and the purpose was to decide which was the best school. There was a big crowd because the reputation of both was at stake.

The fight between Saigo, a small 22-year-old and Kochi, a large and mature man, has become one of the most famous in judo history. At first they looked ill-matched, because Saigo looked so young and so small. Kochi grabbed his opponent, pulled him forwards, and attacked with uchimata. Saigo was swept right up into the air and looked certain to be thrown flat on his back. But at the last second he managed to twist out like a gymnast, and landed on his feet.

Having felt Kochi's strength, Saigo knew he had a hard task on his hands. Kochi got hold of him again and attacked with tai-otoshi. Saigo only just managed to avoid it. He spent a little while avoiding the powerful hands of Kochi, but knew that at some point he had to come to grips with at least trying to win the match.

By this time, the huge Kochi was getting angry. He felt the smaller man was making a fool of him, but he felt very confident. He attacked with osoto-gari, then harai-goshi, and each time he swept Saigo into the air, but each time the small man wriggled off the throw. Yet Kochi never seemed in danger.

Then Saigo seized Kochi's jacket and moved left and right with speed, trying to bewilder his opponent. He attacked with ouchi-gari and Kochi nearly fell backwards. Kochi reacted by using brute force to heave Saigo into the air. Once again the gymnast landed on his feet.

It was at this point, as Kochi stood there amazed at his opponent's escape, that Saigo attacked with his favourite technique – yama-arashi or mountain storm. His compact frame darted in underneath Kochi, turned smoothly, and catapulted Kochi into the air and on to his back. Contemporary reports indicate that it took some time before Kochi managed to get to his feet.

Saigo had won, and Kodokan Judo became the leading school in Japan.

The dojo in Eishoji soon became too small and Kano had to move to a larger hall. By now he had become a university teacher – he spoke perfect English – but he spent much of his free time teaching and practising judo.

When he started to travel abroad he taught judo at every opportunity. Once, when he was on a ship, he was explaining his basic ideas of judo and was overheard by a huge Russian wrestler. The wrestler challenged him to a contest and Kano – who by now was an important man – agreed. He bowed to the wrestler and immediately threw him with uki-goshi (sliding hip) which was his favourite technique.

The Russian didn't know what was happening – except that he was suddenly flying through the air and about to land hard on the deck. People watching saw Kano actually put his hand under the Russian's head so that he shouldn't bang it on the hard wood.

Jigoro Kano came to Europe and taught judo there. Gradually, clubs began to open in England, France, Germany, America and many other countries.

One of the first Japanese judo men who came to England to live was called Yuko Tani. Like Dr Kano he was quite small but very skilful – he could defend himself against much bigger men. There were no clubs where he could teach or practise, so he toured the music halls, challenging anyone to try and beat him. He was prepared to give his opponents £50 if they could beat him. That was a lot of money in the early 1900s. No one could.

Eventually he settled down and became one of the teachers in England's first judo club, The Budokwai, in London. It is still a top club today, and has been the home of such leading international competitors as Brian Jacks and Neil Adams.

Judo changed quite a lot in the early days. At first, many judo students learned punches and kicks as well as throws and other techniques. But there were still a lot of injuries. Eventually all blows, and other techniques like leglocks, were banned, making judo safer than ever.

In 1938, Dr Jigoro Kano died – returning home on a ship called *The Hikawa Maru*. But by that time judo was truly international.

In 1964, judo was seen for the first time in the Tokyo Olympics. It was very popular. There were three weight categories – lightweight, middleweight and heavyweight – and an open weight category, which fighters of any weight could enter. Although Japanese fighters won the three weight categories, a huge Dutchman, Anton Geesink, won the open category.

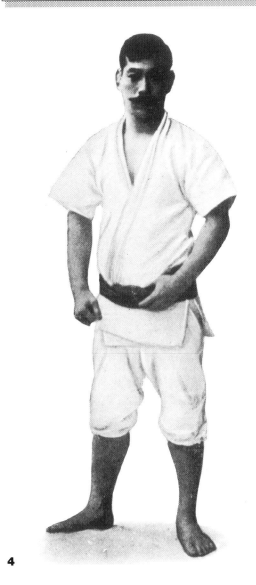

4

Yukio Tani (1881-1950)

This showed that judo was a combat sport for the world, not just for Japan.

Most countries in the world have judo clubs. There are judo clubs all over Europe, in Africa, in the towns and the mountains of India, in South and North America, in China, in Russia and Australia. There are many judo clubs in Japan – hundreds of thousands of young boys and girls do judo in schools all over Japan.

And all because one teenager didn't like being bullied.

CHAPTER TWO

The dojo and its etiquette

The dojo is the training hall. In Japan, dojos can be very beautiful – and very big. You remember that Jigoro Kano's first dojo was just big enough to have eight mats. The Kodokan in Tokyo now has 500 mats and there are even bigger dojos in Japan. The International Budo University – Kokusai Budo Daigaku to give it its Japanese name – has two dojos, with 250 mats each.

The Budokwai, Europe's oldest club, has two dojos, the largest with 80 mats. The High Wycombe Judo Centre, one of the most modern, has 150. The atmosphere can be very special. Judo is good fun, but it is serious as well, and you can feel this in the air. It can be more difficult to get a good atmosphere in a public sports hall where other sports are going on at the same time. Sometimes, you can have an equally good atmosphere in an old church hall – even if the building is not very beautiful, the feeling is good.

5

7

Above: The interior of the main dojo at the International Budo University in Katsuura, a town near Tokyo

Above right: Another typical Japanese dojo

Right: The main dojo at the International Budo University, Japan

6

Left: A junior class in The Budokwai, London

Below: Some of the Kodokan rules and the taiko, the drum which exists in almost every dojo in Japan. When it is time to change partners, one of the students beats the drum

8

TATAMI – THE MATS

The Japanese word for mats is "tatami". They were originally made out of rice straw with a specially woven surface. It was quite hard to land on, but it was better than landing on a bare wooden floor or a concrete pavement.

Now mats are made of special foam and plastic so that the landing is quite soft. In all dojos in Japan, and some dojos in England, the floors are "sprung" – they have springs or rubber underneath the floorboards. This means that even if you are thrown high in the air you can land without getting hurt – with the help of proper breakfalls.

Lots of other kinds of mats – canvas mats and jigsaw mats and gymnastic mats – are also used for judo.

O-TAIKO

In the corner of all the main dojos of Japan there is a large drum called o-taiko. The drum is beaten with a heavy drumstick to mark the beginning and end of every practice, which generally lasts five minutes. The sound echoes around the dojo.

BOWING AND ETIQUETTE

When two Japanese meet, they don't shake hands – they bow. This is why, in judo, we bow.

Jigoro Kano felt it was very important to be polite at all times, but particularly in the dojo. If two people are trying to throw each other or hold each other on the ground, it is easy for one to lose his or her temper. Perhaps one of them will get so angry he will punch his partner, which is how fights start. Kano thought this was bad for judo, so he insisted that everyone had to bow, and it is a tradition observed throughout the world.

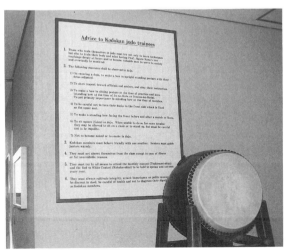

9

REI – THE BOW

"Rei" means bow in Japanese. There are two kinds of bow, the standing bow and the kneeling bow.

Standing bow – tachi rei
Stand with your feet together and hands at the side. Bow by bending at the hips, not the waist (see figs. 10 and 11).

Kneeling bow – za rei
Kneel with your feet flat, but your body upright, and hands on your thighs. Bend forward, putting your hands flat on the ground in front of you. You don't have to bend so far down that your head touches the ground. Halfway down is enough (see figs. 12 and 13). But try not to let your bottom stick up in the air.

WHEN TO BOW

When you enter the dojo
In Japan, you bow when you enter the dojo. If you have just rushed in from school or from the street, a short bow will quieten you down a bit.

Many dojos follow this rule in the rest of the world too. If the club is not in a separate building but a mat in a sports centre, you can bow as you step on to the edge of the mat.

10

11

12

13

At the beginning and end of the class

Most judo sessions begin and end with a kneeling bow between the teacher and the pupils. This is a mark of respect. The pupils are thanking the teacher for teaching, and the teacher is thanking the pupils for coming to the class (especially if they arrive on time with their belts tied correctly!).

Try, sometimes, to be the first to arrive or the last to leave. You bow to an empty, silent dojo. It may even be dark. The dojo has a very special atmosphere then – and it means that you can do extra long training.

At the beginning and end of each practice

Every time you have a new partner, you must bow to each other, at the start and the finish. If you are practising your throws or are doing standing randori, you must bow standing up. If you are doing ground work, you must bow kneeling down.

You must bow to your partner, even if you don't particularly like them. If they have just thrown you rather hard, you may be thinking, "Next time I get hold of you I am going to dump you on your back with my favourite tai-otoshi." But you must bow.

Of course, judo is about fighting. But Jigoro Kano wanted people to be able to develop throwing and fighting skills without hurting others. That is why judo is a polite combat sport, and why etiquette is very important.

Everyone bows. Even when world champions practise with beginners, they bow. And when world champions are about to fight each other in the final of a big competition, they bow.

When you leave the dojo at the end of a practice, you bow. In a way, you are saying "thank you" to the dojo. As you can see, there is a lot of bowing in judo.

CHAPTER THREE

The kit

● The judo kit is called "judogi". There is a white jacket with long sleeves and a white pair of loose trousers. A belt is tied around the waist to hold the jacket together (see fig. 14).

Some people say they look a bit like pyjamas but they are very different because they are designed as fighting kits, not sleeping kits!

The jacket is made of thick material because it has to take a lot of pulling and pushing. That is why they are stronger than karate kits, though it doesn't matter so much for juniors if they have a lighter kit, because the pull on the jackets is not so strong.

Even though the kits are made to take great stress and strain, they do sometimes tear, especially when they get a bit old – or when the fighters are very powerful.

In one international competition between a Japanese and a Russian, they tore four kits between them before the Japanese, Sumio Endo, threw the Russian flat on his back. But this doesn't happen very often.

When girls wear ordinary jackets in the West, they close them right over left, in the opposite way to boys. But in judo, we follow the Japanese way, which is left over right. There is no difference between boys and girls – at least in the way they fold their jackets! The only difference is that girls wear t-shirts under their jackets. In competition, the t-shirt must be plain white, but in ordinary practice it doesn't matter so much.

The trousers are slightly lighter than the jackets, but they are also strong. There is a special draw-string to keep them up.

The traditional colour for judogi is white. But in recent years, in Europe, there has been a new fashion for blue judogi. In some international competitions, one fighter wears a white kit and the other a blue kit – it helps to distinguish between them. Sometimes, if both are wearing white, it is difficult to see who is doing what to whom.

Some of the best judogi are made in Japan, but these can be very expensive. Some of the leading competitors have judo suits made especially for them, so that they fit very well.

14

But most people wear judogi that feel comfortable and are quite loose. The sleeves should come down to the wrists, and trousers to the ankles.

At first, wearing a judogi feels strange. But after a little while, it feels the most comfortable clothing you will ever wear.

CLEANLINESS

The judoka – the Japanese word for the person who does judo – should be neat and clean. It is not very pleasant to practise with someone with a smelly judo kit or smelly feet! Your kit should be washed regularly . . . and so should your feet!

THE JAPANESE KIMONO

The traditional Japanese dress with wide sleeves. The lapels cross over and are held in place by a belt.

THE BELT

The belt is very important in judo. It is called "obi" in Japanese. It is like a sign, because the colours mean different grades. Therefore, it should be tied very neatly – and the better it is tied, the less likely it is to come undone.

All belts should be tied in a neat reef knot, with the

15

16

17

18

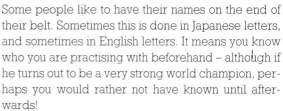

ends equal. After a little practice, this becomes very easy.

1. Hold the belt in front of you in both hands (fig. 15).
2. Put it around your waist, and bring the ends to the front. Hold one end in each hand (fig. 16).
3. Fold the end in your right hand over the left (fig. 17).
4. Slip it under both lengths, and give it a little tug. This is the halfway point. Your hands are now holding the other ends (fig. 18).
5. I now fold the right-hand end over the left and pull sideways on both to make the reef knot (fig. 19).
6. The finish (fig. 20).
Simple, huh?

NAMES ON BELTS

Some people like to have their names on the end of their belt. Sometimes this is done in Japanese letters, and sometimes in English letters. It means you know who you are practising with beforehand – although if he turns out to be a very strong world champion, perhaps you would rather not have known until afterwards!

Generally, people wait until they get their black belt before putting their name on their belts.

ZORI

Although it is not part of the main judo kit, it is useful to carry around a pair of sandals. These are used to walk from the changing rooms to the mat. It is easier to slip into sandals, rather than go to the trouble of putting shoes on and off every time you leave the mat. No one should ever walk barefoot on the ordinary floor and then step on the mat, because it makes the mat dirty.

The traditional Japanese footwear is called zori. They are sandals with thongs, and are made partly out of straw. They look very nice, but don't last very long – especially if you get caught in the rain!

19

20

CHAPTER FOUR

The grades

Do you want to get a black belt? There is one very easy way. You go to the nearest sports shop and you ask the shop assistant what your size is in judo belts.

She may say: "Size 3".

Then you say: "Please can I have one size 3 black belt?"

You give her the money and she will give you the belt. It's very easy. But it is not very satisfying.

The other way is more difficult. You join a judo club. You train every week there for a number of years. You learn your breakfalls. You learn your throws and holds. Sometimes you get knocks and bruises. Sometimes you lose competitions.

There will be club nights when you want to stay in and watch television, or go out with your friends. But you don't – you pick up your judogi bag and walk off to the judo club.

Every week, every month, you get a little stronger, a little bit more skilful with your seoi-nage or your tai-otoshi. You may not even see your own progress – but your instructor does. He or she is watching you improve, encouraging you when things don't seem to be going very well, giving you advice and help. Often, when you do a good throw, he will see it out of the corner of his eye, even if he doesn't appear to notice.

The white belt you were given when you first started judo gradually changes colour, to yellow, orange, green. After some months at green belt you will suddenly remember how, in the early days, you would face an orange belt and think to yourself: "Good breakfall practice coming up . . ." But now orange belts are quite easy to throw, and even easier to hold down.

And one day, if you don't give up, you find you are a brown belt entering a grading. You are able to answer all the theory questions comfortably and demonstrate all the throws smoothly and correctly. Then you have your contests – five or six other brown belts all out to beat you.

It is hard going, but you feel strong. You notice that the other brown belts are breathing heavily, but you are fit and moving well and you know that the long period of training has paid off.

You throw some of your opponents. Others you hold down – or defeat with armlock or strangle-hold. You have done all that is required, and the senior instructor announces that you are graded to black belt, first dan.

The very next morning you can go into your local sports shop. You won't need to ask the shop assistant your belt size, because you know it already. All you will have to say is: "One black belt, size 6, please."

THE GRADES

The special coloured belt system is one of the special features of a dojo. Walk into most dojos in the world and you will see a mixture of grades on the mat.

There are a number of reasons why judo introduced the coloured belt system. Here are two of them.

The first is to show how much experience you have had in judo; the second is to show how little experience you have had in judo.

If a black belt asks for a randori with another black belt, then he knows he can go as hard as he likes.

But if he is practising with a green belt, then he knows he must be a little more gentle. He must not only throw the green belt, but encourage him too. He can let the green belt throw him, and even offer a little advice with his techniques if there is something obvious that needs correcting. This is true throughout the grading system. The senior grade must always respect the inexperience of the junior grade.

And remember, it is not a good idea for a green belt to start telling a black belt what he is doing wrong!

21

THE GRADES AND THEIR BELTS

The junior grades

Most countries and judo organisations in the world have slightly different systems for their junior gradings, but the basic ideas are much the same.

In Britain, the official judo organisation is the British Judo Association. The grading system devised by the BJA for 8-15 year-olds is as follows.

The junior grades are divided into 18 sections called "mon grades". For each mon you have to learn one new throw, one new ground work technique and one new referee's call in Japanese.

The grades are indicated by a particular belt and by red coloured bars on the belt

The mon grades

1st mon :	White belt + one red bar.
2nd mon :	White belt + two red bars.
3rd mon :	White belt + three red bars.
4th mon :	Yellow belt + one red bar.
5th mon :	Yellow belt + two red bars.
6th mon :	Yellow belt + three red bars.
7th mon :	Orange belt + one red bar.
8th mon :	Orange belt + two red bars.
9th mon :	Orange belt + three red bars.
10th mon :	Green belt + one red bar.
11th mon :	Green belt + two red bars.
12th mon :	Green belt + three red bars.
13th mon :	Blue belt + one red bar.
14th mon :	Blue belt + two red bars.
15th mon :	Blue belt + three red bars.
16th mon :	Brown belt + one red bar.
17th mon :	Brown belt + two red bars.
18th mon :	Brown belt + three red bars.

Mon means "gate" in Japanese. These grades are like gates you have to pass through to get to the house of black belt judo.

The theory grading examinations

Here are some examples of the kind of things you will need to know for your grades:

Beginner to 1st mon   Throw: ogoshi. Ground work: kesa-gatame. Referee's call: Hajime.

1st mon to 2nd mon   Throw: kouchi-gari. Ground work: kami-shiho-gatame. Referee's call: Matte.

2nd mon to 3rd mon   Throw: ippon-seoi-nage. Ground work: yoko-shiko-gatame. Referee's call: Osaekomi.

10th mon to 11th mon   Throw: seoi-otoshi. Ground work: ude-garami (an armlock). Referee's call: Hantei.

17th mon to 18th mon   Throw: uchimata. Ground work: Hadaka-jime (a strangle-hold). Referee's call: Hansokumake.

Contests

In addition to the theory, you will have to take part in two or three contests to show that you can put all this theory into practice. You must be able to do judo, not just talk about it. Sometimes lower grades will beat a high grade in a contest; for example, a green belt may beat a blue belt. This doesn't necessarily mean that the blue belt is no good at all. It may mean that the blue belt is very good at demonstrating and not so good at contest, while the green belt is good at fighting but has difficulty remembering one throw from another. The grades are not just about contest, but the complete understanding of judo.

This even applies to black belts. Sometimes black belts can be beaten by brown belts, though it doesn't happen very often. The Japanese understand this. They say: "Even monkeys fall off trees."

SENIOR GRADES

The senior grade system is much the same – except without the tabs. The sections are divided into kyu and the numbers go in descending order.

White belt		Black belt	
9th kyu:	Yellow belt.	1st Dan:	Black belt.
8th kyu:	Orange belt.	2nd Dan:	Black belt.
7th kyu:	Orange belt.	3rd Dan:	Black belt.
6th kyu:	Green belt.	4th Dan:	Black belt.
5th kyu:	Green belt.	5th Dan:	Black belt.
4th kyu:	Blue belt.		
3rd kyu:	Blue belt.		
2nd kyu:	Brown belt.		
1st kyu:	Brown belt.		

Senior grades

6th Dan:	Red and White belt.
7th Dan:	Red and White belt.
8th Dan:	Red and White belt.
9th Dan:	Red belt.
10th Dan:	White belt.

Neil Adams, who won the world light middleweight title in 1981, two Olympic silver medals and six European titles, became a sixth dan the year after he retired from competition in 1989.

Here is Ann Hughes about to start a competition. The white belt she is wearing is to distinguish her from the other black belt opponent

22

George Kerr from Edinburgh, an eighth dan

23

Karen Briggs, who has won four world bantamweight titles, and five European titles, is a fifth dan.

So is Ann Hughes, world lightweight champion in 1986.

To achieve these titles not only did they have to be good at competition, but they also knew their theory very well, and demonstrated kata.

In Britain, there are about six eighth dans. There are many more eighth dans in Japan. There are also a few ninth dans, and one tenth dan. There have been less than 10 tenth dans in judo history.

Jigoro Kano, the founder of judo, wore a black belt, but did not have a grade. There was no one to grade him.

Warming up and breakfalls

STRETCHING AND WARMING UP

Every judo class in the world starts with some stretching and warming-up exercises. If you don't, there is a chance of straining muscles.

There are lots of different exercises you can do. Here are a few:

1. Run on the spot, getting your knees high, or run in a circle if you have the room: 50-100 steps (fig. 24).
2. 10 star jumps (fig. 25).
3. Stand with your legs apart, and twist, looking behind you to the left and then to the right: 3 times each side (fig. 26). Make big circles in the air with your arms: 5 times one way, 5 times the other, to loosen your shoulders.
4. Put your hands on your hips and make big circles with your hips: 5 times one way, 5 times the other (fig. 27).

5. Keeping your legs straight, touch the ground in front of you with both hands, then between your legs, then lift your hands and arch backwards: 5 times (figs. 28 and 29).
6. Bring your feet together. Put your hands on your knees and take your knees in a circle: 5 times one way, 5 times the other (fig. 30).
7. Touch your toes – but don't cheat: keep your knees straight! Do it 3 times (fig. 31). If you can't reach your toes, don't despair. Bend from the hips as far as you can go. Do this 5 times every morning when you get up and just before bed and you will be able to touch your toes easily within a month – and probably sooner.

24

25

26

27

28

29

30

31

Breakfalls

How do you feel about being thrown approximately one metre up into the air and falling down to the mat (see figs. 32 and 33)? Not very happy about it? Well, not many boys or girls are. Most adults are even more worried about it than juniors – after all, they are much heavier and think they will make an even bigger SPLAT! Breakfalls solve the problem.

When Jigoro started judo as a teenager, no one taught breakfalls and you had to learn as you went along. Often, young people didn't break their falls – they broke their bones instead. That is why he insisted that everyone must be taught proper breakfalls.

It is not a great secret – it just takes a bit of practice.

After a short while you find that if you trip up in the playground by accident, you will be able to do your breakfall and roll to your feet without a bruise.

32

33

34

35

Ukemi

Ukemi is the Japanese word for breakfalls. Ukemi will be your first judo technique, so you should learn the Japanese word for it.

Rear breakfall

The first breakfall you learn is the rear breakfall. You can learn this in two stages.

FIRST STAGE: Lie on your back, bend your knees, and hit the mat with both hands. As you hit the mat, bring your hips off the ground: 5 times (figs. 34 and 35).

SECOND STAGE: Crouch down. Now roll easily backwards like a ball (see figs. 36 and 37). As your back rolls to the ground, hit the mat with both hands. You can let your legs go right over the top. Then return to the crouch and start again: 5 times. With practice, you will be able to throw yourself backwards and land in this perfect position.

Now come the two main breakfalls. You do one on your right and one on your left. So, here's the Japanese: right – migi; left – hidari.

In Japanese, right breakfall is migi ukemi; left breakfall is hidari ukemi. Simple, isn't it? You can learn these side breakfalls in two stages.

36

Migi ukemi

FIRST STAGE: Lie on your back, bend your left knee, turn very slightly on your right side, raise your head a little, and bang the mat with your right hand. You should hit the ground all the way up your arm – not just the hand: 5 times (fig. 38).

SECOND STAGE: Crouch down. Poke your right leg out in front of you (fig. 39) and, as you fall to the side, bang the ground with your right hand. Don't forget to keep your head tucked in. If you don't, it can snap backwards.

38

39

Hidari ukemi

FIRST STAGE: Lie on your back, bend your right knee, turn very slightly on your right side, raise your head a little and bang the mat with your left hand (fig. 40). You should hit the ground all the way up your arm – not just the hand: 5 times.

SECOND STAGE: Crouch down. Poke your left leg out in front of you (fig. 41) and as you fall to the side, bang the ground with your left hand. Don't forget about the head.

40

41

Rolling breakfalls

These are a more advanced kind of ukemi. But you'll be able to manage them quite easily.

You learn them on the left and right – you never know which way your partner will throw you.

Right-hand rolling breakfall

1. Put your right foot forward. Stretch out with your right arm (fig. 42). Tuck your head under, and over you go (fig. 43). As you roll over on to your back, hit the ground with your right hand (fig. 44). Smile.

2. Put your left foot forward. Stretch out with your left arm (fig. 45). Tuck your head under, and over you go. As you roll over on to your back, hit the ground with your left hand (fig. 46).

TIP: Imagine you are going right over your head like a forward roll. At first it can feel odd doing it with just one arm, but you will get used to it, and you won't go over sideways.

If you watch higher grades in the dojo, you can see they are being thrown all over the place and still bounce back up again.

Warning: Breakfalls are very good, but they have their limitations. For a quick exit from an aeroplane, please use a parachute. Jigoro Kano did not design ukemi to be used from 5,000 feet.

42

43

44

45

46

The throws

47

48

GRIPS

To throw your partner, the first thing you have to do is to get hold of him or her. It is very, very difficult to throw someone without taking hold. To do that you have to be better than a world champion. You have to be a magician – or at least a star in a martial arts movie.

You can hold your partner's jacket more or less anywhere, but these are the best ways – at least until you start going up the grades and getting experienced.

Don't forget to bow.

● Stretch out your right hand and take your partner's lapel (fig. 47).
● Stretch out your left hand and take your partner's sleeve (fig. 48).
● Your partner can do the same to you (fig. 49).

This is called the basic right-hand grip.

49

KUZUSHI – breaking of balance

With this grip, you can unbalance your partner in different directions.

● You can unbalance him to his right (fig. 50), to his left (fig. 51), backwards (fig. 52), and forwards (fig. 53).

Each of the throws you are going to learn needs one of these breaks of balance. It is difficult to throw someone who is well-balanced.

Now you are ready to try and throw each other. This is where the fun of judo really starts.

50

51

52

53

OGOSHI (major hip throw)

This is almost the same as the throw used by Jigoro Kano to beat the huge Russian wrestler on the ship. You can lift a much heavier school friend with it quite easily. But don't try Mum or Dad until you get used to it – and they learn how to breakfall!

1 Pull your partner on to his toes (fig. 54).
2 Let go with your right hand, but keep him on his toes. Slip your arm around your partner's waist as you step in (fig. 55).
3 Bring your hip right through and pull your partner on to you (fig. 56).

4 Rock him off his feet. You can test your control by taking a few steps with your partner on your back (fig. 57).
5 Throw him. You can give him a little support with the sleeve grip so that his landing is not too hard (fig. 58).

You can walk around the dojo with your partner on your back to get the feel of carrying someone on your hip – and make sure you have good control.

54

55

56

57

58

IPPON-SEOI-NAGE
(one-arm shoulder throw)

This is a very popular throw in competitions.

1 Face your partner. Hold your partner's right lapel. The traditional method is to hold the sleeve, but this is more difficult in modern judo. Pull him off balance with the lapel grip (fig. 59).

2 Turn in by stepping across with your right foot and tucking your left foot in behind you. Look at the left arm movement in the picture. There is a strong pull on the lapel which brings the partner just off his heels. Tuck your right arm under the bicep (fig. 60).

3 Bring your partner on to your back. The literal translation of the Japanese word for this throw means "back carry". Notice how the knees are bent and the thrower is ready to drive forwards (fig. 61).

4 The throw (fig. 62).

Both ogoshi and ippon-seoi-nage are throws you can use if you happen to be attacked on the beach – you don't need to get hold of a jacket!

59

60

61

62

MOROTE-SEOI-NAGE
(two-arm shoulder throw)

This is the most popular throw of all among juniors throughout the world. It is very satisfying, because if you get right under your partner, you can take her high into the air and (very) flat on her back.

1 Pull your partner off balance to the front (fig. 63).

2 As you step in, twist your right arm under her arm (fig. 64).
3 With your knees nice and springy, take her into the air (fig. 65).
4 And throw . . . giving a little support at the end (fig. 66).

63

64

65

66

67

Above: A perfect ippon-seoi-nage

Right: Here is morote-seoi-nage done by a Japanese champion in an international competition. He has adjusted it slightly and has gone down on one knee to get low under his opponent. There are many other variations of morote-seoi-nage, including going down on both knees. Have you noticed that this champion is throwing to his left?

68

DE-ASHI-BARAI (advanced foot sweep)

This throw doesn't need any effort at all. It is just like sweeping a room clean.

1 You are walking across the mat (fig. 69).
2 Just before your partner puts his weight on to his right foot, you sweep it away (fig. 70).
3 Then you pull down with the hands (fig. 71).

When you sweep a floor, you don't sweep it with the hard "ankle" part of the broom. You use the softer bottom part. And it's the same with de-ashi-barai. Clashing ankles hurts!

69

70

71

72

Above: This is Yasuhiro Yamashita, world and Olympic champion and the most successful Japanese competitor ever. Here he is throwing with de-ashi-barai in a practice at London's The Budokwai

73

74

75

76

OSOTO-GARI (major outer reap)

This is particularly good if you have got long legs, but a shorter person can do it effectively too.

1 The start (fig. 73).

2 Step towards your partner, pulling him off balance so that all his weight is on his heel (fig. 74).

3 Then bring your leg through, lifting it quite high like a swingboat in a fair – then bring the leg down, toes pointed, against your partner's leg (fig. 75).

4 This action enables you to take your friend off his feet and high into the air (fig. 76).

KOSOTO-GARI *(minor outer reap)*

Osoto-gari, the one before this, means major or large outer reap. Kosoto-gari means minor or small outer reap. "O" at the beginning of a Japanese word means "big" or "major" and "ko" means little or minor or small.

But even though it is small, it will still throw your partner. You can use the same leg, but you attack your partner's other leg.

1 The start (fig. 77).
2 Step slightly to the side of your partner (fig. 78).
3 Tip your partner slightly backwards and scoop her foot off the ground. Now, with the bottom of your foot and your leg you can sweep your partner right off her feet and on to her back (fig. 79).

77

78

79

TAI-OTOSHI (body drop)

So, you want to trip up your friend (. . . on the judo mat only!). This is the best way to do it. It takes two steps, and then the trip.

1 Take one step across your partner's path, pulling him forward a little (fig. 80).
2 Bring the other foot round so that you are both facing in more or less the same direction. Don't forget to keep pulling (fig. 81).

3 Now your leg can dart across and trip up your partner (fig. 82).
4 Keep pulling him over (fig. 83).

If your friend is going to be caught by the trip, he must be coming forward or at least leaning forward. He isn't stupid and he won't trip over your leg if he sees it in front of him. He will just stop walking. So, continuing the pull with your hands is VERY IMPORTANT.

80

81

82

83

KOUCHI-GARI (minor inner reap)

This is another "small" technique – look, the word begins with "ko". But it can flatten very big men, so long as you get the timing right. Otherwise it will feel like kicking a lamp-post, which will hurt you both.

1 You face your partner (fig. 85).

Below: Diane Bell gives a fine demonstration of left kouchi-gari. Note the way Diane has turned her foot to sweep with her sole, her perfect timing and committed attacking posture

2 Step back on your left foot (remember – hidari in Japanese), and pull your partner with you so that you are moving together. It is a bit like dancing – at first, you are both moving at the same time. But at the end of the step you have to go a bit faster, because your left foot touches the ground before your partner's. Immediately, you sweep across with your right foot (fig. 86).

3 It is broom time again. Sweep – you can even try and make your partner do the splits. Then it is easy to push him on to his back (fig. 87).

84

85

86

87

88

89

90

OUCHI-GARI (big inner reap)

Now the big one. You can charge into your partner when you do ouchi-gari. It is a bit like pushing a wall down. It takes two steps and a reap.

1 Step in front of your partner with your right foot. Bring your left foot a little closer – you want to make a triangle with your left foot and your partner's feet (fig. 88).
2 Slip your right foot in between your partner's legs as in the photo – it shouldn't be difficult, because your partner can't see what you are doing . . . Lean into your partner a little to break his balance backwards (fig. 89).
3 Trailing your big toe on the ground, reap him off his feet, and, with your hands, steer him on to his back (fig. 90).

TSURI-KOMI-GOSHI (lift-pull-hip)

This is not an easy throw. You need to be quite flexible to get in position. But when you get it right, your partner rolls right over your hip.

1 Face to face (fig. 91).
2 Step in with your right foot, pulling your partner off balance (fig. 92).

3 Bring your body round by tucking the left foot in behind. Stick out your hip – your partner is going to roll over it as if she was going over a bar (fig. 93).
4 The throw – you can control your partner all the way to the mat (fig. 94).

91

92

93

94

95

96

97

98

HIZA-GURUMA (knee wheel)

You have to think you are driving a big bus with a big wheel in your hands. Note that this is shown in the photographs with a left-hand grip – you don't have to do everything right-handed.

1 Face to face (fig. 95).
2 You step to one side to get a bit out of your partner's way (fig. 96).

3 Stick out your foot and put the sole just below your partner's kneecap. Don't put it on the kneecap because if you kick you may hurt him (fig. 97).
4 Now, imagine that you are turning your bus to the right (fig. 98).

Try looking over your right shoulder: this helps to keep the big wheeling action going.

HARAI-GOSHI (sweeping hip)

What's your balance like? Can you hop comfortably on one leg without toppling over? You need to be good on one leg for this throw.

1 Face to face (fig. 99).

2 Step across, pulling your partner so that he is tipping on to the toes of his right (migi in Japanese) foot (fig. 100).

3 Step around with your other foot so that you are facing in more or less the same direction. Make sure your feet are very close together (fig. 101).

4 Holding him close to your body, you now become a seesaw. Down goes your head and his chest. Up goes your leg – with your friend on the end of it (fig. 102).

99

100

101

102

103

104

105

UCHIMATA (inner thigh throw)

Uchimata is used in senior competition more than any other. It calls for very good balance as can be seen from this example by Neil Adams in the 1980 Olympics, where he won a silver medal.

1 He is poised on one foot as he tries to lift his opponent off the ground (fig. 103).
2 He goes even higher on to his toes in order to get more lift. At this moment, his opponent must have felt it was the beginning of the end (fig. 104).
3 Neil pulled him right round on to his back – Ippon (fig. 105).

106

Above: Here is another example of uchimata, this time from Ingrid Berghmans, the great Belgian world champion. She was losing this match against Barbara Classens (West Germany) but with only a few seconds to go she pulled off this brilliant uchimata for ippon to win the match and the 1987 European title

107

108

109

TOMOE-NAGE (whirl throw)

110

111-114. This is Britain's world champion Karen Briggs demonstrating tomoe-nage. She won her first world title with this throw, and has thrown every top opponent with it, including champions from Japan, France, the Soviet Union and the USA

This is one of the most famous of all judo throws. The Japanese call it a "sutemi waza", which means "sacrifice technique" because you "sacrifice" your own body position in order to throw your opponent. There are many variations to it – but everyone starts with this one.

1 Face to face (fig. 107).

2 Step in with your left foot, keeping your knee slightly bent (fig. 108).

3 Put your foot up in your opponent's stomach – don't kick! Now just sit down close to your heel, pulling your partner over your head (fig. 109).

4 Now she will not be able to stop rolling over you on to her back (fig. 110).

These are only a few of the many judo throws you can learn. There are dozens of others. Some have very poetic names such as yama-arashi (mountain storm) or tsubame-gaeshi (swallow counter). One successful contest throw is called tani-otoshi, which means "valley drop" – because your partner feels he is being dropped into a deep, deep valley.

111

112

113

114

115

Left: Karen Briggs in action with her tomoe-nage again – this time throwing Barbara Eck (Austria) on her way to winning the European title in 1986

Combinations and counters

COMBINATIONS

Judo throws can be easy, especially if your partner doesn't know what's coming. The trouble is that your partners have probably had the same lessons as you, and they know the throws just as well. Sometimes (when you are feeling a bit tired) you'll attack so slowly that your partner can see it coming a mile off and avoids it easily.

Even when you are quite fast, your partner may be feeling like a 100-metre sprinter, and is up and away before you have managed to turn into position.

This is where the combination tricks are so useful. You attack with one throw and make your partner believe you are really trying to throw with it.

He then tries to stop it.

And you are waiting, like a lion in the grass, with another throw.

Kouchi-gari into morote-seoi-nage

This has got to be fast and smooth. If it looks like a film it will work. If it looks like lots of different holiday snaps it will not.

1 Tap your partner's foot as if you were going to do kouchi-gari (fig. 116). She thinks "Pathetic, really pathetic", and steps off it.
2 You immediately twist in for morote-seoi-nage (fig. 117).
3 As she flies through the air she is probably still thinking, "Pathetic, really pathetic" (fig. 118).

116

117

118

Ouchi-gari into tai-otoshi

This is a great favourite in Japan. Lots of boys and girls use it. So when you go to Tokyo on holiday, and you visit the local judo club, watch out for it.

1 Attack with ouchi-gari (fig. 119).

2 Don't be upset when your partner steps off it and says: "Is that the best you can do?" (fig. 120).

3 Bring your left foot round and switch to tai-otoshi (fig.121).

4/5 Shoot your leg across and throw with a clean tai-otoshi. That is the best you can do! (figs. 122 and 123).

119

120

121

122

123

Kouchi-gari into ouchi-gari

This is a really tricky one. You go for one leg, he takes it away, so you go for the other one.

1 You attack with kouchi-gari. Your partner has seen this a million times before, and just steps off it (fig. 124).

2 But he's a bit more careful now, because the last time you did that was too casual and you threw him forward with morote-seoi-nage. So he leans back a bit (fig.125).

3 The answer is easy. You bring your left foot round a bit (fig. 126).

4 And switch to ouchi-gari (fig. 127).

124

125

126

127

128

Hiza-guruma into harai-goshi

This is a difficult one – and only for those who are good at balancing first of all on one leg and then on the other. If you wobble badly on one leg and you try this, you will probably end up with your partner in a heap on the floor. When you can do it, and if you keep going to judo as you get older, you will probably end up a black belt.

1 Attack with hiza-guruma, trying to wheel your partner round. He leans a little, but not enough to be thrown – and stops the attack (fig. 128).
2 Quickly bring your leg back to the mat, but turn so that you face the other direction. With your partner still leaning slightly you can attack with harai-goshi (fig. 129).
3 Now, sweep him off his feet (fig. 130). Not easy, huh?

129

130

Russian world
champion Grigory
Veritchev attacks with
harai-goshi, having
first attacked with
hiza-guruma

131

132

133

COUNTERS

If your partner attacks you with a technique that is not very good, he will probably be a bit unbalanced. It is quite easy to throw someone who is wobbly, so why don't you go straight into the attack there and then?

Tsubame-gaeshi

This technique has a very beautiful name -tsubame gaeshi means "swallow counter". It looks very, very simple. But it has to be as quick as a swallow changing direction in the sky – yet smooth and well-timed.

1 Your partner attacks you with de-ashi-barai (fig. 134).
2 You feel it coming, and simply lift your foot out of the way, bending at the knee (fig. 135).
3 Now your swallow foot darts back on the attack, capturing your partner's foot. And over she goes (fig. 136).

It is really de-ashi-barai countered by the de-ashi-barai.

134

135

136

137

Osoto-gaeshi

This is much the same idea – you use the same throw to counter with.

1 Your partner attacks you with osoto-gari. But he hasn't bent you backwards at all (fig. 137).

2 So you take a little step with your left foot (fig. 138). (It may be a small step but it is important. If you don't take it you may find yourself flat on your back. Don't say I didn't warn you.)

3 Now you can reap him off his feet (fig. 139).

138

139

140

Ogoshi countered by ogoshi

This is all about flexible hips, and is fun to practise.

1 Your partner attacks you with ogoshi. You avoid the attacking hip and step in front of your partner, sliding your hand around your partner's waist (fig. 140).
2 Now you can attack with ogoshi – but it is a left-handed attack. You must get your hip well across your partner's front (fig. 141).
3 Once you have jacked her up in the air, you can throw (fig. 142).

141

142

Tai-otoshi countered by kosoto-gari

You have to be quite relaxed to do this, and good at stepping over legs.

1/2 Your partner attacks with tai-otoshi (figs. 143 and 144).

3 Don't trip over the outstretched leg – step over it as if you were stepping over a very low fence (fig. 145).

4 Now turn to face the way you have come, and, reaping with your leg, push your partner on to her back (fig. 146).

143

144

145

146

147

148

149

150

Ouchi-gari countered by tomoe-nage

This is not quite as simple as it looks, but it can come as quite a surprise to your partner. Remember – only do it when your partner can do good rolling break-falls. When you practise it, make sure there is no one behind you on the mat – otherwise there will be a collision!

1 Your partner attacks with ouchi-gari, but you step off it easily (figs. 147 and 148).

2 You bring that left leg around and put it in front, in between your partner's legs. This is important. (Don't try and put it right up into his stomach, because you will just fall in a heap.) Now you are going to change legs. Stand on your left leg and bring your right leg up into your partner's stomach (fig. 149).

3 This is the time to go down to the ground and throw with tomoe-nage (fig. 150).

CHAPTER EIGHT

Ground work

Newaza

Ground work is the second half of judo. If you throw your opponent flat on his or her back in a competition there is no need to go into ground work. The competition would end there and then, like a knock-out punch in boxing.

But sometimes – in fact, quite often – you lose a little control and your opponent lands on his side. Or he manages to twist in the air so that he doesn't land flat on his back.

Then you have to follow up with ground work. The Japanese word for ground work is "newaza". Three different kinds of techniques are used in newaza: holds, armlocks and strangles.

Most juniors only practise holds, because armlocks and strangles can be a bit dangerous. In most competitions around the world, you have to be 16 before you are allowed to use armlocks or strangles. So this chapter will concentrate on holds.

There is a special Japanese word for holds : osae-komi.

The holds

The purpose of osaekomi in a judo competition is to hold your partner on his or her back for 30 seconds. Your friends can wriggle around and try and escape – and if you are caught in a hold that is exactly what you have to do.

But if you have put the hold on properly, your friend should not escape. You could hold him or her down for longer than 30 seconds if you wanted. You could hold them for a minute or two minutes or an hour. You could hold them down as long as you wanted, until Christmas. But 30 seconds is generally long enough.

There are many different kinds of holds, each with special names. Here are six.

152

Above: Here is Brian Jacks, Britain's first competitive 6th dan, smiling as he wins the All-England Championships in 1977

Left: Kesa-gatame is used by judoka of all ages. Here is an eight-year-old boy winning his competition in Japan with it

Kesa-gatame (scarf hold)

This is a friendly hold. You have one arm around your partner's neck and you can talk to her. You could ask her how she is getting on with her escape from the hold – though your judo teacher would probably not be very pleased with the noise.

1 Sit down beside your partner as in fig. 153.
2 Put your right arm around your partner's neck and hold on to her collar (fig. 154).
3 Tuck your partner's right arm under your armpit and hold tight. Spread your legs – and sit tight (fig. 155).

153

154

155

Kata-gatame (shoulder hold)

If your partner manages to get her arm free, this is what you do with it.

1 The arm slips out.
2 You push it across the face – you should push the elbow (fig. 156).
3 Then you link hands and hold tight. This is not very pleasant for your partner (fig. 157).

156

157

Kami-shiho-gatame (upper four quarters hold)

This is a completely different kind of hold, as you can see from the pictures. Your partner's head can get a bit squashed.

1 Kneel down just in front of your partner's head (fig. 158).

2 Slide the back of your hands along the mat and under your partner's arms (fig. 159).

3 Grab the belt and hold tightly, squeezing your partner's arms. Turn your head to the side so that it lies on your partner's stomach. You should be able to hear all the activity inside. Now stretch out your legs, spreading them a bit.

Some tips may be useful. Keep your hips down on the ground, but keep your toes turned under. Although you are lying flat, you want to be alert, not like a flat pancake (fig. 160).

When you first try this hold, ask your partner to squirm one way and then another. This will give you a good idea of what it is like to hold someone who is really trying to escape.

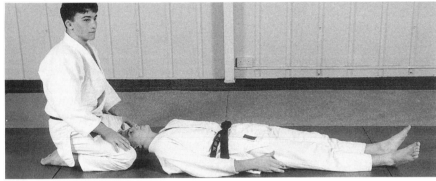

158

159

160

Kuzure-kami-shiho-gatame (broken upper four quarters hold)

This may be a bit of a mouthful to say, but it is a very strong hold – one of the strongest in judo. Not many people can escape from it.

1 Start like kami-shiho-gatame. Now let go of the belt with your right hand and curve it under your partner's arm (fig. 161).

2 Bend it round so that it comes up to the back of his neck. Hold the collar tightly (fig. 162).

3 Slightly adjust your position so that rather than squashing the head you are slightly off to one side. Now you can squeeze tightly with both hands. The hold is on (fig. 163).

161

162

163

164

165

166

Yoko-shiho-gatame (side four quarters)

When you are fighting in ground work it is not often you can get up to the head of your partner. It is much easier to get to the side – which is why this hold is popular.

1 Kneel by your partner's side (fig. 164).
2 Put your right arm around her neck and hold the jacket tightly. Make sure there is no gap between your arm and her neck (fig. 165).
3 Lie on her. Imagine what it feels like if a mattress is put on top of you. Well, this is what you must feel like to your partner – a mattress lying on top (fig. 166).
4 Put your left hand between your partner's legs. You can hold the seat of the trousers or even the belt if your arms are long enough; or the bottom of the jacket as in the photo. But don't slide your body down towards her legs. It should be chest to chest at the top. Finally, spread your legs like a tripod to give you good balance (fig. 167).

Tate-shiho-gatame (lengthwise four quarters hold)

This is a bit like horse-riding.

1 Sit astride your partner, with your knees and legs close against her side. Lean forward and put your right arm around her neck (fig. 168).
2 Capture one arm and push it across her face. Push against the arm with the side of your head. Clasp your hands together and squeeze a little. This is exactly like the top half of kata-gatame (fig. 169).

Now ask your partner to struggle as hard as she can. She will bridge up, and it is your job to keep her body down as much as you can, and not topple over. Ride it, cowboy!

168

169

167

TURNS

It is really easy to put a hold on a friend who is lying down for you. It is much more difficult to do it when your friend is trying to put a hold on you at the same time. Here are some ways of doing it.

In competition you go from standing down to ground work without a break. But in judo classes in the dojo you generally practise throws and ground work at different times.

Turns from the back

Often, during competition and club practice, your partner will end up in a defensive position on all fours. She doesn't want to be turned on her back where she can be held down.

But it is your task to do precisely that. It can turn out to be a bit of a chess game, with each of you trying to outwit the other. This is one of the best games in judo.

There are many turns in judo – not even the top champions or the old Japanese masters will know them all. And new ones are being invented all the time. Neil Adams won the world championships in 1981, beating Japan's champion Jiro Kase with an arm-lock – just because he had developed his own particular turn.

Here are three turns. They can be slotted together like a jigsaw. You start with one, and if that doesn't work you can go on to another; and if that doesn't work, try the third.

170

First arm roll

1 Kneel down beside your partner and slide your left arm underneath her chest until you can grab the arm. Now slide the other arm under the chin and hold your own hand (fig. 170).

173

Second arm roll

1 Your partner knows what you are going to do, so she puts her arm away. Don't panic, or wish you had longer arms. Put your left hand in and take hold of the jacket-lapel, fingers inside, thumb outside (fig. 173).

171

2 Now give the arm a strong pull and nudge the body with your chest (fig. 171).

172

3 Over goes your partner, and you can slide into yoko-shiho-gatame (fig. 172).

174

2 With your right hand reach around the face and take hold of the sleeve. Don't just pull. You must pull in a circular motion. And at the same time you must push with the other arm (fig. 174).

175

3 Pull right round and look to your right. This will bring your partner right over on to her back and you can hold her easily in kesa-gatame (fig. 175).

Third roll

But what happens if your friend knows this one, too? Simple.

1 Slide your hand in and take the lapel in the same way as before. Your partner will then stretch out her free hand, and then pull it in and keep it moving so that you can't get hold of it. Don't panic. Slide the fingers of your right hand inside the back of the collar – fingers in, thumb out (fig. 176).

2 In the second roll, you turned to your right. Now you are going to turn to your left. Look over your left shoulder and stick your left leg along her side (fig. 177).

3 Roll to the left, and as your partner rolls on her back, prepare to mount her like a horse (fig. 178).

4 You are now in tate-shiho-gatame. All you need to do is sort out the arms (fig. 179). Tuck the legs in.

176

177

178

179

Turns from between the legs

This is a very common situation in judo. It is the job of the person on his back to be very clever and turn his partner and hold him down.

But it is the job of the person on his knees to get past the legs and hold his partner down.

Let's deal with the one on his back first. Here are two turns.

180

First turn

1 Sit up a bit and take hold of the sleeve and lapel (fig. 180).
2 Bend your left leg well and place it on your partner's knee (fig. 181).
3 Push away the knee as you pull hard with your hands (fig. 182).
4 Your partner will overbalance and you can turn him on his back (fig. 183).
5 Then it is easy to go into a hold – yoko-shiho-gatame, for example (fig. 184).

181

182

183

184

185

186

187

188

Second turn

This is a bit trickier. You will have to follow the instructions carefully.

1 Sit up (fig. 185).

2 Wrap your left arm around his right arm and go across his chest with your hand to hold his left lapel. OK? Just practise that a few times, because it is a bit complicated (fig. 186).

3 Now slip your right leg under his left leg. Get your foot under his shin so that you can lift it a bit (fig. 187).

4 As you can see, the idea is to whip him over on to his back with your legs acting like scissors (fig. 188).

5 As soon as you have done that, you can sit up into tate-shiho-gatame, or even kesa-gatame if you prefer (fig. 189).

189

190

DETAIL: Here is the turn from the other side. Note the scissoring action with the legs (figs. 190 and 191).

191

Getting past the legs

But what happens if you are the one between the legs? Here are a couple of ideas.

ATTACK 1

1 Grab your partner's trousers. With your left hand, push down on the inside of your partner's knee (fig. 192).
2 Kneel over it – a little gently, so that your partner doesn't end the practice with a big bruise (fig. 193).
3 Now, maintaining the pressure, go over the legs. Keep up the pressure with your left knee. This will stop him sitting up and trapping your right leg (fig. 194).
4 Clear the right leg (fig. 195).
5 Finish with yoko-shiho-gatame (fig. 196).

192

193

194

195

196

ATTACK 2

1 Slide back a little (fig. 197).

2 Put your right hand under one knee as in the picture (note the knuckles), and take hold of the other trouser-leg around the knee if you can (fig. 198). Flatten out on your stomach.

3 Wriggle round (fig. 199).

4 Use the same method to put pressure on your partner's leg to stop him trapping your leg (fig. 200).

5 Now you can go into yoko-shiho-gatame (fig. 201).

197

198

199

200

201

Freeing the trapped leg

Sometimes you have done all the hard work. You have turned your partner on to her back from the all-fours position. You have got into a hold. But then she traps one of your legs which, under judo rules, means that the hold is not properly on. In a competition, the hold is only on, and the 30-second count-down started, when both your legs are free. So, you have to learn how to free your leg, even when your partner doesn't want you to.

FREE THE LEG
1 You are holding in kesa-gatame, but your right leg is trapped. Pull yourself up your partner's body with your arms (fig. 202).
2 Use your other leg to push and push while you pull and pull with the trapped leg (fig. 203).
3 Eventually, it will come free and you can put on kesa-gatame (fig. 204).

202

203

204

Osaekomi – holds – are a very important part of judo. You must get very good at holding people down. You must also learn to escape from holds when you are held down, and not to give up struggling.

Your instructor may show you armlocks in your club, though you won't be able to use them in competition until you join the senior ranks. But you have to put them on very carefully, otherwise you can injure your partner.

You will also learn how to use strangles. These can be very dangerous, because if they are not carefully controlled, your partner can become unconscious.

See fig. 205 for an example of a strangle in a competition.

SUBMISSION

In ground work, you can always submit by tapping the ground or your partner twice. It is important to tap quickly and in good time if a strangle or an armlock is going on. You can also tap if you are caught in a hold, but you must struggle and try very hard to get out first of all.

In his autobiography *A Life in Judo*, Neil Adams remembers what happened after he caught Kase on the ground:

"We tumbled over and over three times and each time he slipped his head from under my leg. Eventually, he settled on to his back and like all supple Japanese players, he attempted to bridge out of my grip.

"I gritted my teeth and fought to force his arm up towards his head, just far enough to break his grip, but not far enough to allow him to bridge out and escape.

"We were on the floor for what seemed like an age but in reality was only about 40 seconds. I was desperately trying to get his hand out and I remember seeing his fingers starting to pull and slide and I could see they were losing their grasp . . .

"I kept thinking: 'You've done it, you've done it.' After his fingers had released, and I was trying to put the armlock on, I suddenly thought: 'Oh God, he is not going to tap.' Then I saw his little hand come up and he tapped. I could have kissed him – but of course I didn't. At last I was champion of the world; I raised my arms in triumph and the British contingent popped their champagne corks."

206

Above: Nick Kokataylo of England strangles Joe Meli of Canada into submission in the final of the 1986 Comonwealth Games

Left: Here is Neil Adams winning his world title in the world championships in 1981 in Maastricht, Holland, armlocking the Japanese champion, Kase

Practice

● If you are learning the piano or the trumpet you have to practise your scales every day, or at least regularly during the week. If you want to be a champion swimmer, you can't just splash around in the pool. You have to go to the swimming pool early in the morning a few days a week, to get fit and improve your swimming technique.

And it is the same with judo. If you want to get really good at it, you must practise.

The Japanese practise a lot. That is why their judo is so good. Neil Adams and Karen Briggs practised a lot when they were teenagers. They were awarded their black belts when they were very young – Neil was 15 and Karen 16. It was not surprising that they grew so strong and became world champions.

There is no other way. If you sincerely want to be good, you must practise regularly – and well. Being a good fighter is not enough. You must have good technique as well.

IN THE DOJO

It is difficult to practise judo outside the dojo. There are some things you can do at home which will be listed later. But most of the practice must be done in the dojo.

FITNESS

You don't have to be superfit or as strong as an ox to do judo. You will be OK as long as you can run around an athletics track without needing an oxygen mask at the end. And if you can do basic rolls, and carry the family shopping home on Saturday – then you are agile and strong enough.

The rest you can develop in the dojo. Later on, if you start going seriously into competition, you will need to do extra fitness training: running most days, stretching so that you can almost do the splits, and eventually doing weight training. But that is for your late teens.

JUDO TECHNIQUE

What you really need to do now is develop your judo technique. You must get quite good at demonstrating all the throws and holds in this book. And you need to know their names in English, and even Japanese, if you can manage it.

But although you should be able to demonstrate the techniques, you will probably only use a handful of them in the fighting practice that you do. These will be your favourite techniques. In Japanese, the word is "tokui-waza".

All the world champions, whether they are English or French or Russian or Japanese have their "tokui-waza". They will have spent many years and thousands of hours developing them so that they can throw most people in the world with them. They know that if they visit a dojo in Paris or Rome or Vienna or Moscow or Bombay or Tokyo, they will use those three or four throws more than anything else.

At first, you will try lots of throws. But after a while you will realise that you like some throws best of all.

UCHIKOMI

The best way to develop throws, and make them really strong, is "uchikomi". This is the Japanese for "entries".

You take a partner and attack with, for example, ippon-seoi-nage. You turn in and get nicely under your partner, breaking his balance every time. Then come out again. This enables you to practise your

207

208

209

entries and get them very smooth. It is like a pianist doing his scales.

You can do them in sets of 10 or 15 or 20. Then you have a breather and it is your partner's turn. When he has finished, it is your turn again.

This way, you can do many repetitions without actually throwing.

It can be quite tiring, but you will soon get used to it.

1,000 SETS

There is a traditional Japanese practice, called the 1,000 Sets. You need to be quite fit and strong and determined for this, so you may have to wait until you are at least a blue belt. But everyone can do 100 Sets or 200 sets.

1 Take 10 pebbles in to the dojo. Put them beside the mat.
2 Decide on a technique. Your partner decides on a technique.
3 Do 100 uchikomi on your technique – say ippon-seoi nage. Then pick up a pebble, run to the dojo door, and throw the pebble away. Run back to your partner.

4 It is his or her turn. Don't forget, think about what you are doing. Don't just go on to automatic pilot, doing uchikomi like a machine. Concentrate on the left hand for 25, the right hand for 25, the left leg for 25, the right leg for 25. Or leave the last 10 for the whole body movement. Keep your mind alert.
5 Do your second 100. And so on, until you have completed 1,000. There is a tradition in Japan that until you have done 100,000 uchikomi on a particular throw, you haven't begun to understand it.

UCHIKOMI ON THE MOVE – TIMING

You don't have to practise uchikomi standing still – although generally it is a good idea to start with some static uchikomi.

You can do it with your partner taking just one step in a particular direction. Or two steps or more. This helps to develop not only your entry, but your timing as well.

Timing is really important. You know what it is like if someone in an orchestra clashes the cymbals at the wrong time. It sounds awful. It is the same in judo when the timing is out: you bump into the wrong bits, bruise something and fall over.

210

TIMING FOR IPPON-SEOI-NAGE

Here is one example of timing, although there are many – even for one throw.

1 Your partner steps backward with his right foot (fig. 210).

2 You step forward, slightly at an angle. You should move more or less at the same time as your partner, so that you develop a smooth flow.

3 Then, before he can move again, you complete your entry, getting into a good throwing position (fig. 211).

4 Then you both return to the starting position and do it all over again.

You could do this many times without getting tired. This is how smooth good judo can be.

NAGE-KOMI (throwing repetition)

You also have to practise throwing. It is good for the person doing the throwing and also lets the person being thrown practise breakfalls.

211

You can throw three times, and then let your partner throw three times. Then it is your turn again, and so on.

RANDORI (free practice)

This is the best fun in judo. This is where you try out all the skills you have learned. You bow to your partner, your partner bows to you – and then you try and throw each other. It is fighting fun. Some things will work and your partner will be whisked over on his or her back. Some things will not, and you will clash legs. Sometimes your partner will attack well and over you go, producing a magnificent breakfall.

Everyone wants to do well in randori, but it doesn't matter if you are thrown. Randori is the time to experiment. Even world champions get thrown in randori. They do their breakfall, get up, and start again (though then they try even harder to throw their partners! World champions don't like getting thrown).

So, don't worry if you find yourself doing breakfall after breakfall. Some boys and girls find throwing easy; some find it difficult. But more often than not the people who win in the end are those who stick at it.

GROUND WORK PRACTICE

And don't forget you must do your ground work uchi-komi as well.

You can do arm roll 1 five times. Then it is your partner's turn.

You can hold your partner in kesa-gatame and see if he can escape.

You can let your partner hold you in yoko-shiho-gatame and see if you can escape.

TRAINING PARTNERS

It is very helpful to have a good friend to practise with. Of course, you must practise with lots of different people, because you must get used to doing throws on people bigger than you, smaller than you, the same size, older and younger.

But it is nice doing judo with a special friend.

PRACTICE AT HOME

It can be difficult doing judo practice at home. There is always Mum or Dad, of course. You can get Dad to stand in the living room before breakfast for 10 minutes or so while you do your uchikomi. But don't do any throwing – he may land and hurt himself because he doesn't know how to breakfall!

You can also get Mum to lie on the ground and see if you can hold her in kesa-gatame. See if you can switch to kami-shiho-gatame without letting her escape.

You can try it on brothers and sisters too. But carefully. You don't want to throw your little brother on the hard floor. And even if you want to throw your big brother on the hard floor, it may not be a very good idea! He wouldn't be very happy about it!

SHADOW UCHIKOMI

You can also do some training yourself in your own room.

212

You can practise your reaping action, against a wall like this. Make sure you get a powerful leg movement, and that the toes are pointed (see figs. 212 and 213).

You can also practise other movements. Stand in the middle of the room and just practise your stepping patterns.

Imagine you are holding a partner. At first, it feels a bit strange. But just as a violinist must practise his scales on his own before he joins an orchestra, so it helps for a judoka to practise his or her steps before he gets hold of a real live partner.

In any case it is good to practise with an imaginary partner, because you can always win!

SPECIAL PRACTICES

In the hottest part of the summer in Japan, and the coldest part of winter, there are special judo classes. They are designed to forge the spirit of the judoka.

The summer practice is called Shochu Geiko. It is held in the full heat of the early afternoon. Even to move is an effort, and to keep up a fast judo practice is not easy. No water is allowed. The practice can last for two or three hours.

The winter practice is called Kan Geiko. It is held at 5 a.m. The windows of the dojo are opened. The heating is not turned on, and no track suits, socks or other warm clothing is allowed. It is bitterly cold and you can see your breath in the biting morning air.

Japanese teachers feel that if you can last a week or more of these hard practices, you can probably cope with most hardships in life.

But for Jigoro Kano, judo was not so much about winning championships, but developing skilful judo – and a strong and heroic personality.

213

Below: These Japanese students have already done 2½ hours of judo in the heat of the summer. But they have not finished. They end their practice with 30 minutes of physical exercises – including shinning up ropes to strengthen their grips

Rules and scoring

■● The original rules and scoring for those who studied ju-jitsu were very easy to learn. They were the rules of the battlefield, and samurai warriors understood them very quickly: you were allowed to do anything.

The scoring was very simple too: if you won, you lived. If you lost, you didn't.

But, thankfully, things have developed a bit since then, and it doesn't matter so much if you make a mistake or if you come across a person who is bigger, better or stronger than you. You just lose points and perhaps a bit of pride.

RULES IN THE DOJO

Jigoro Kano wanted to make judo a safe combat sport. When he started learning ju-jitsu, there were not many rules and many people were injured.

When he opened his school, Kodokan Judo, he made a number of rules. First of all, there was to be no kicking or punching in ordinary randori. He thought it was difficult to practise throwing techniques if, every time you grabbed hold of your partner, you were punched on the nose. Kano knew that if he was in a real fight, then he could avoid or block the punch, then grab the opponent and throw.

But during ordinary lessons in the dojo, he didn't want a lot of punches or kicks flying around.

Another important reason for this was that Kano wanted his students who learned judo to become strong and good at self-defence; but also polite. He didn't want his students to feel that they could go around hurting people. He wanted them to be quiet heroes and heroines. So one of the first rules in the dojo was no kicking and punching.

In the very early days of Kodokan Judo, everyone learned leglocks as well as armlocks and strangles. But too many people received bad knee injuries, and

so leglocks were banned in competition. As a result, they are not practised in normal randori, though sometimes in special training they can be studied. In many countries, most juniors are not even allowed to use armlocks in competition until they are 16, although sometimes they can practise them in the dojo very carefully.

In 1894, Kano wrote 14 rules for his Kodokan Judo. They were mostly about behaviour – all his students had to be very well mannered.

The first rule was: "Those who do judo must pledge to benefit the state and mankind through the training of their bodies."

Among the other rules were the following:

Only if they were ill or had another good reason could they miss the practice.

Advanced students had to look after and help the beginners.

In the dojo, all students had to sit or stand correctly – no slouching, lying around or leaning against the walls.

Students who lived in Tokyo had to present their teacher and judo friends with one piece of "kagami-mochi", a Japanese rice cake, at New Year.

The final rule was: "Conform to the true spirit of judo:

● always foster a sincere heart
● respect morality
● discharge your duties
● be prudent in your conduct
● be hygenic
● and, with regard to all things, be of right mind."

There are many other smaller rules, almost always for safety's sake. For example, you mustn't put your fingers or thumb inside your partner's sleeves or up the trouser-leg. The reason for this was that too many fingers were getting caught and snapped like dry twigs.

CONTEST RULES AND SCORES

The aim of judo competition is to win by "ippon". You throw your partner so that he or she lands flat on the back. IPPON!

You can also hold your partner in a hold for 30 seconds. IPPON!

Seniors can put on a strangle and when the opponents submit, IPPON!

Seniors can put on an armlock and when the opponets submit, IPPON!

The idea behind these scores is: if it happened in a real fight in the street, who would win?

If someone is thrown flat on his back in the street, the force of the landing would be so hard he wouldn't be able to get up. That is like ippon in the dojo.

If someone is held on the ground for 30 seconds, he would probably never escape. That is like ippon in the dojo. And if someone was armlocked or strangled

This is the referee's signal for ippon

and didn't submit, they would be badly injured. That is like ippon in the dojo.

As you can see, judo competition is based on a real fighting situation.

SMALLER SCORES

However, it can be difficult to get a clear ippon in competition. So smaller scores were introduced to make a clear winner. It can seem a little confusing at the start, but this list should make it reasonably clear:

- Ippon = 10 small points
- Waza-ari = 7 small points
- Yuko = 5 small points
- Koka = 3 small points

WAZA-ARI

You know how to get ippon. Well, waza-ari is the score below ippon. If you throw your opponent half on his back, the referee will give you waza-ari (7 points).

If you hold your partner for 25 seconds, the referee will give you waza-ari. If you get two waza-aris, it adds up to ippon.

Of course, judo people can add up, and they know that 7 + 7 = 14. And 14 is more than 10. And 10 small points make ippon. But you don't get anything extra for those four more points.

The reason for this is that if you threw an attacker twice on the pavement and he landed half on his back, he may get up from the first one but he probably wouldn't get up from the second one. You would be able to walk home and make a cup of tea without any further interference.

So, remember, one waza-ari followed by another waza-ari is just ippon.

YUKO

If you throw your partner on to his side, you will be awarded yuko (5 points).

If you hold your partner on the ground in a proper

216 This is the referee's signal for waza-ari

217 This is the referee's signal for yuko

218 This is the referee's signal for koka

hold for 20 seconds, you will get yuko (5 points).

BUT . . . yukos do not add up.

The reason for this is simple. If you were attacked in the street and you threw the attacker for a yuko, he would probably get up and have another go at you. He would probably think you were lucky.

You could probably throw him all night with one yuko after another, and each time he would get up, a little more bruised than before, but still keen to have another go at you.

So, in a contest, even if you get 25 yukos and you are bouncing your partner around the contest mat like a yoyo, they don't add up to ippon. All he needs is one waza-ari, and he could win.

KOKA

If you throw your partner so that he lands on his bottom, you will score koka (3 points).

If you hold your partner on the ground in a proper hold for 10 seconds, you will score koka (3 points).

BUT . . . if you score 50 kokas, they will not add up to ippon. You know the reason – it is the same as yuko scores.

If you score 5 kokas, but your partner scores one yuko, your partner will win.

PENALTY SCORES

There are also four penalty scores if you have broken important rules.

Hansokumake means "disqualification". You must do something pretty bad for this. If you argue with the referee, you can get hansokumake – which is one reason why very, very few judo contestants argue with referees.

- Keikoku is a seven-point penalty.
- Chui is a five-point penalty.
- Shido is a three-point penalty.

You can be given these penalties for a number of things, including being passive (just walking around and not trying to throw your partner) and putting your fingers in your partner's jacket. Don't!

DRAWS

If there is a draw between two fighters – if they have both the same score or no score at all – the referee and two corner judges will decide who tried hardest to win.

OTHER CONTEST RULES

Most contest rules are just common sense.

One rule says that the two competitors must start standing up, and they can only go into ground work after a small throw or if they fall over having tried to throw each other.

If this rule didn't exist, judo competitions could start with people lying flat on the floor because they didn't want to be thrown. Perhaps they were not very good at their breakfalls. This wouldn't be very much fun at all.

CONTEST TIME

International and most senior contests last five minutes for men and women.

Junior contests can be shorter, sometimes as little as two or three minutes. So you must try your best for all that time . . . it's not very long.

JAPANESE CONTEST WORDS

You have to understand some Japanese words to take part in a judo contest:

- Rei – Bow.
- Hajime – Begin.
- Matte – Break. The referee may call matte if the belt of one of the contestants becomes undone and is about to trip up its owner.
- Osaekomi – The hold is on. The referee calls this when the hold is on and the table official can start the 30-second count (see fig. 219).
- Soremade – That is all. The referee calls this at the end of a contest, when the time is up.

219

THE MODERN COMPETITION SCOREBOARD

1 It shows the time, which works on a count-down to 0.
2 The board is divided into two, red (the competitor wearing a red belt, in addition to his black belt) and white. Red is on the left on the board.
3 The scores. As you can see in fig. 220, waza-ari is at the top, yuko in the middle (white has scored a yuko) and koka at the bottom. There is no ippon, because the contest is over when ippon is scored.
4 There are also the penalty scores. These are shown on the outside of the board – keikoku, chui and shido. If a competitor incurs a penalty, a coloured light goes on beside the penalty.

220

Competition

● Every Olympic champion started as a boy or a girl in a small judo club, competing in the local competition. Many of them lost their first fights, but didn't mind so much because they enjoyed the judo. They went into a few more competitions, and gradually they started winning.

Jigoro Kano didn't want competitions to be only about winning, especially for juniors. Of course, everyone likes to win. But it is also a good chance to try and make your favourite techniques work without making any mistakes. The more you can do this, the stronger you know your techniques are becoming.

Competition also shows you where your weaknesses are. Maybe you find that you are throwing your opponents, scoring yuko or waza-ari, but then they are beating you on the ground. If you are always getting caught in holds, then you know you must improve your ground work.

This is exactly what happened to Neil Adams. When he was a teenager he threw most people with morote-seoi-nage and tai-otoshi and other throws. And his ground work wasn't too bad.

But in one competition, in the British Open in 1978, he was caught on the ground by a Frenchman and strangled. This made him realise that he needed to practise more ground work.

The following day, he went to his judo club and began to practise ground work very seriously. He made a special study of juji-gatame, the armlock. From that day to the day he retired from competition, he won many gold, silver and bronze medals, including one world championship gold medal, two Olympic silver medals and six European gold medals. He lost a few competitions – but he never lost in ground work. No one ever held him down or armlocked him or strangled him in competition ever again.

So, Neil Adams learned one of his best lessons by losing a competition.

When he was in secondary school, his father – who was himself a judo black belt – used to take him to a few competitions. But not very many.

JUNIOR COMPETITIONS

Going to competitions weekend after weekend and twice on Sundays is very tiring. And often it doesn't let young people develop their techniques. They feel they must win, rather than try out the throws and holds they are trying to develop.

But competitions can be fun. Although boys and girls practise together in the dojo, they have separate competitions, as in all other sports.

Most competitions are organised in weight categories. These vary in junior competitions, but the weights generally start around 25 kilos.

SENIOR COMPETITIONS

In the senior events, there are seven weight categories for the men and seven for the women.

Men's weight categories
Bantamweight (under 60 kg)
Featherweight (under 65 kg)
Lightweight (under 71 kg)
Light middleweight (under 78 kg)
Middleweight (under 86 kg)
Light heavyweight (under 95 kg)
Heavyweight (over 95 kg)

There is also one extra category in some competitions:
Open weight

Women's weight categories
Bantamweight (under 48 kg)
Featherweight (under 52 kg)
Lightweight (under 56 kg)
Light middleweight (under 61 kg)
Middleweight (under 66 kg)
Light heavyweight (under 72 kg)
Heavyweight (over 72 kg)

221 Some people will grab anything to stop themselves being thrown

There is also one extra category in some competitions:
Open weight

NERVES

Almost all competitors get a little nervous before a competition. They get butterflies in their stomachs. Sometimes they feel more like giant insects from the Amazon jungle.

Neil Adams admits: "Sometimes I have felt so nervous before a big competition that my legs felt weak and I could hardly walk on to the mat. But the nerves generally disappeared after the first match."

Here are some of the important international competitions in the world:

Olympic Games
World Championships
European Championships

British Open
Tournoi de Paris
Hungary Cup
American Open
Tiblissi Open (Soviet Union)
Shoriki Cup (Japan)
Kano Cup (Japan)
All-Japan Championships – just for Japanese competitors; there are no weight categories.
Asian Games.

The European championships are held in a different country each year. Recently, it has been in Belgrade (Yugoslavia) 1986; Paris 1987; Pamplona (Spain) 1988; Helsinki (Finland) 1989; Frankfurt (Germany) 1990; Prague (Czechoslovakia) 1991.

Judo has been in six Olympic Games: Tokyo (Japan) 1964; Munich (Germany) 1972; Montreal (Canada) 1976; Moscow (Soviet Union) 1980; Los Angeles (USA) 1984; Seoul (South Korea) 1988. It will be in Barcelona (Spain) in 1992.

SOME FAMOUS CHAMPIONS

Men

Anton Geesink (Holland) Olympic champion 1964
Isao Okano (Japan) Olympic middleweight champion 1964
Wilhelm Ruska (Holland) Olympic heavyweight and open champion 1972
Shozo Fuji (Japan) four times world light middleweight champion
Vladimir Nevzerov (Soviet Union) Olympic lightweight champion 1976
Nobuyuki Sato (Japan) world light heavyweight champion 1967, 1973; All-Japan champion 1974
Jean-Luc Rouge (France) world light heavyweight champion 1975
Angelo Parisi (France) Olympic heavyweight champion 1980
Neil Adams (Britain), world light middleweight champion 1981
Katsuhiko Kashiwazaki (Japan) world featherweight champion 1981
Yasuhiro Yamashita (Japan) Olympic open champion 1984 and world champion 1981, 1983

Michael Swain (USA) world lightweight champion 1987

Elvis Gordon (Britain) European open champion 1988

Women

Karen Briggs (Britain) world bantamweight champion 1982, 1984, 1986, 1989

Ingrid Berghmans (Holland) Olympic demonstration champion 1988; world champion 1982, 1984, 1986, 1989

Brigitte Deydier (France) world middleweight champion 1982, 1984, 1986

Diane Bell (Britain) world light middleweight champion 1986, 1987

Sharon Rendle (Britain) world featherweight champion 1987, 1989

Ann Hughes (Britain) world lightweight champion 1986

Kaori Yamaguchi (Japan) world featherweight champion 1986

Fenglian Gao (China) world open champion 1986, 1987, 1989

Cathy Arnaud (France) world lightweight champion 1987, 1989

Loretta Doyle (Britain) world featherweight champion 1982

KAREN BRIGGS

222

Karen Briggs is one of the most successful judo competitors ever. Although she is under five feet tall and very often weighs considerably less than 48 kilos, she has won the world bantamweight title four times – an extraordinary achievement.

The first time was in Paris, in 1982, when she was just 19. She used her famous yoko-tomoe-nage, and threw the Japanese champion in 20 seconds. The fourth time was in Belgrade, Yugoslavia. Karen had suffered a very bad accident in the world championships in Essen, breaking her leg. But after months in plaster, and nearly a year of careful recovery, she came back to competition. In Belgrade she held down the Japanese champion, Fumiko Esaki, in less than a minute, even though she dislocated her shoulder while she was doing it.

Karen is regarded as one of the best all-round fighters in judo. Her favourite throws are tai-otoshi, tomoe-nage and ouchi-gari, and she is very strong on the ground, particularly with holds.

She also loves running, cycling, swimming and playing football. When she was six, she wanted to become a professional footballer – until she discovered judo.

DIANE BELL

223

Diane Bell came from the small town of Craw-crook, near Newcastle. Ann Hughes came from Liverpool. They met when they became members of the British women's squad. They were both British champions, Diane at lightweight and Ann at light middleweight. But they couldn't win the world championships.

After one competition, when neither won a medal, they decided to swap weight categories. Diane was taller than Ann, so she went to the under 61 kg category, and trained hard to put on muscle; Ann went on a diet to get down to under 56 kg.

At the next world championships, in Maastricht, Holland in 1986, on the same day, they both won their categories to become world champions. In Diane's final against the French champion, she was behind on attacks although there had been no score. But on her very last attack, one second before the bell, she scored a koka with ouchi-gari, and took the world title. "You must never give up, no matter how tired you are. You must fight right to the bell."

At the next world championships, in Essen, West Germany, Ann won a bronze, but Diane won the gold medal again.

SHARON RENDLE

224

Sharon Rendle is another British champion to win the world title twice – in 1987 and 1989. Sharon was born in Hull but moved to Grimsby and is the star of the Grimsby Judo Club. She specializes in morote-seoi-nage. In the first round of the world championships in Essen, in 1987, she threw her American opponent just seven seconds after the start of the fight for ippon with morote-seoi-nage.

Sharon has also used footsweeps – which helped her win the gold medal in the Olympics in Seoul, 1988 , when women's judo was a demonstration event.

NEIL ADAMS

Neil Adams has been the most successful competitor in men's judo from Britian. He grew up in Coventry and originally wanted to become a professional footballer, but judo took over. He won the British junior title from 1969 to 1973, and became European Espoir (under-18) champion in 1974 when he was 16.

He went on to win the British Open eight times, and the European championships six times. But he became world famous when he won the world light middleweight title in 1981 in Maastricht, Holland, armlocking Jiro Kase (Japan) in the final.

The Japanese already knew how strong he was – in his first competition in Japan, in the Kano Cup, when he was still a teenager, he threw their champion Nishida for ippon.

"I attacked with tai-otoshi, but Nishida just stepped over it. So I attacked again, and Nishida thought I was going to do tai-otoshi again. But I didn't. I changed to uchimata and Nishida was caught in mid-air, and went over on to his back."

Neil went on to win two Olympic silver medals. In Moscow, 1980, he lost on a decision, and in Los Angeles he was thrown for ippon by Frank Wieneke (West Germany) with ippon-seoi-nage. It was the first time Neil had ever been thrown for ippon in a competition in his career.

Since his retirement from competition, he has started his own club, the Neil Adams Club in his home town of Coventry, and has started to coach a new generation of champions.

DENSIGN WHITE

226

Densign White started judo in his school in Wolverhampton when he was 10, and went on to win British junior and senior championships. He was still only a teenager when he competed in his first world championships – in Maastricht, 1981 – and was the top British middleweight for ten years.

Densign was part of a very successful team from Wolverhampton. This included Elvis Gordon, who won a silver medal in the open category of the world championships in 1987, and Dennis Stewart, who won a bronze medal at the Seoul Olympics.

Apart from winning many championships in Britain, Densign won two silver medals in his under-86 kg category in the European championships. His favourite throws include seoinage, tai-otoshi and uchimata – and he is also good at footsweeps. One newspaper called him "the gentleman of British judo", because he fights in a very elegant manner, and he is always polite.

Ian Freeman, who demonstrates many of the techniques in this book, was not quite six when he started judo. "I enjoyed it from the beginning, and although I did other sports at school, judo is the only one I have taken seriously," he says.

Ian started at the Camberley Judo Club with Mark Earle, and still trains there regularly. At first he went once a week, then twice a week, and now he trains almost every day, combining running and fitness work with some weight training, judo technique training and fighting practice. He also enjoys visiting other clubs and will take on everybody, large or small. Because he worked so hard, he got his black belt when he was 16, and the same year won a silver medal in the British Open, a remarkable achievement.

When he did the photographs for this book he was 17.

"I don't know why I love judo so much. It has something to do with the rough and tumble – though at the start there is a lot of tumble and it's not too rough. But it is not just the fighting. There is a lot to learn in judo. There are many techniques, and you have got to know which ones will work at a particular time. Your opponent may be tall or small, fast or strong, left-handed or right-handed, pulling back or pushing forward. In a competition your mind has to work as fast as a computer, sorting out all this information, and then you still have to be prepared to adapt. On top of all that you have to be quite fit – for national and international competition at any rate.

The throw I did in this final was typical. When I attacked, my opponent put his arms around my waist to try and smother the movement, but I just kept on turning. By keeping the circle going, I was able to peel my opponent over on to his back. Technically, it started as a kind of harai-goshi, and then turned into a tai-otoshi. But you don't think about that in competition. You fight as hard and as well as you can, and in this situation you rely on instinct – and all those hours of training that you have done in your own club. On this occasion it worked – it doesn't always!"

IAN FREEMAN

227

228

229

230

TOSHIHIKO KOGA

231

This is Toshihiko Koga, the Japanese world light-weight champion. He has a spectacular morote-seoi-nage, which he can do from just about every position. He also has a very, very fast kouchi-gari.

His opponents try to stop the seoi-nage by leaning backwards. So Koga throws them with kouchi-gari.

If they try to stop the kouchi-gari by leaning forwards, he throws them with morote-seoi-nage. Phew!

Kata

● Many of the old ju-jitsu techniques were so dangerous that it was unsafe to practise them in free-fighting. Instead, the students would practise them in kata form. This meant that they wouldn't be caught by surprise when just practising in the dojo and so they wouldn't get injured.

In judo, kata is a pre-arranged sequence of techniques a little bit like a ballet. Working with a partner, you learn the list of attacks and defences, and then you can perform them at a special event.

To some people, kata can appear a little boring, because it is not as exciting as randori or even uchi-komi.

But if you take the trouble to learn a kata you often pick up little details about a technique or judo generally that help you in your randori and even competition.

For example, when most people practise their judo techniques, they do them either on the right side or the left side. But if your learn nage-no-kata, you must learn to demonstrate the 15 techniques on both the left and the right. There are eight main judo katas:

1 Nage-no-kata – Demonstration of throws.

2 Katame-no-kata – Demonstration of ground work, techniques.
3 Ju-no-kata – Demonstration of softness or non-resistance.
4 Kime-no-kata – Demonstration of decisive techniques.
5 Gonosen-no-kata – Demonstration of counters.
6 Itsusu-no-kata – Demonstration of the five forms.
7 Koshiki-no-kata – Demonstration of antique forms.
8 Goshinjitsu-no-kata – Demonstration of self-defence.

NAGE-NO-KATA

Nage-no-kata is the most popular kata. It has 15 techniques, demonstrated left and right, and is divided into five sections: hand throws, hip throws, foot throws, side sacrifice throws, rear sacrifice throws.

Here are the hand throws. The person who does the throwing is called "tori". The person who is thrown is called "uke".

TECHNIQUE 1 – UKI-OTOSHI

1 First of all tori and uke bow to each other (fig. 232).

2 Tori walks to uke (fig. 233).

3 Uke takes hold and pushes tori (fig. 234).

4 Tori retreats (fig. 235).

5 On the third step, tori kneels down on his left knee, breaking uke's balance (fig. 236).

6 He turns uke on to her back with uki-otoshi (fig. 237).

7 He ends in a strong, balanced kneeling posture (fig. 238).

233

236

237

242

241

234

235

238

240

239

They get up, and start at the other side.

1 Uke takes hold, this time holding with a left grip, and pushes forward (fig. 239).

2 Tori takes hold and retreats (fig. 240).

3/4 On the third step, tori kneels on his right foot and uke is thrown with uki-otoshi (figs. 241 and 242).

Technique 2 – kata-seoi-nage

1 They face each other (fig. 243).

2 Uke attacks tori with a blow which tori blocks (fig. 244).

3 Then tori turns in for kata-seoi-nage. It is very like ippon-seoi-nage, except that he holds the jacket with his right hand (fig. 245).

4 Tori throws uke (fig. 246).

5 Tori gives support, and uke lands in a clean line (fig. 247).

243

246

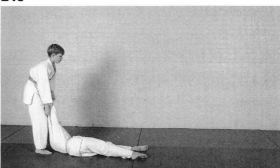

247

251

250

244

245

249

248

1 Uke gets up and faces the way she came (fig. 248).
2 Uke attacks tori with another blow, this time with the
   left fist. Tori blocks (fig. 249).
3 Tori turns in for kata-seoi-nage (fig. 250).
4 Tori throws (fig. 251).

Technique 3 – kata-guruma

1 Starting at the side of the mat (fig. 252), uke takes a right-hand grip and pushes tori.

2 As tori retreats, he takes hold (fig. 253).

3 On the second step, he changes his left-hand grip to underneath (fig. 254).

4 On his third step, he draws uke forward and ducks under his arm (fig. 255).

5 He lifts uke high in the air (fig. 256).

6 And throws.

1 Uke then gets up and faces the way she came (fig. 257).

2 Uke takes hold of tori and tori immediately takes the inside grip (fig. 258).

3 On the third step tori once again ducks under the arm and grabs uke's legs (fig. 259).

4 Tori lifts – with a straight back otherwise he will injure himself (fig. 260).

5 Now he throws uke (fig. 261).

6 They both smarten up, pulling their jackets tight, with their backs to each other. Then they give the final bow to each other – though if they were going on to complete the other techniques, they would not bow until the end (fig. 262).

These are the first three techniques in nage-no-kata. They must be done at an even pace, but not boringly. There must be a lot of vigour and liveliness in the techniques. Uke's breakfalls must be very good. And tori's throwing techniques must also be good. For example, when he does kata-guruma, he must not bend over but maintain a good posture. Details like this improve everyone's judo.

Judo is not only about having a good old scrap!

When Neil Adams took his fifth dan, he had to demonstrate his kata, even though he was a world champion. The same with Ann Hughes, the 1986 world lightweight champion from Liverpool. She had to do the same for her fifth dan.

252

255

259

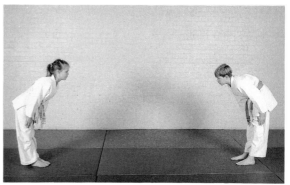

262

253

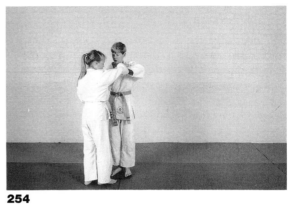

254

256

258

257

261

260

Japan and the Japanese

● You don't need to speak Japanese to do judo. All you really need to do is bow, take hold and throw. But it helps if you do know some Japanese words.

In every country in the world where people do judo, they use Japanese names for the techniques. Sometimes they use their own language too, as we do. Occasionally, we will say "shoulder throw" and occasionally we will say "seoi-nage". It means the same thing.

But if you go to a judo club in France on holiday and you don't speak any French, you can still speak a little Japanese to your French judo friends.

And if you are having a holiday in Mongolia and you don't speak any Mongolian you can go to a judo club and speak a little Japanese.

Of course, if you go to Japan to do your judo, you will have no trouble at all!

SOME JAPANESE WORDS

You have already learned a few Japanese words. Here are some more to help you along.

Tori – in judo, the person who throws
Uke – in judo, the person being thrown
Obi – belt
Sode – sleeve
Te – hand
Ashi – foot (and leg)
Hai – yes
Iie – no
Ohayo gozaimasu – good morning
Oyasumi nasai – good night
Hajimemashite – nice to meet you

Arigato gozaimasu – thank you very much
Coca-Cola o onegaishimasu – can I have a Coca-Cola, please?
Sensei – teacher
Gambatte kudasai – please try your best
Tsuyoi desu – you are strong
Sumimasen – sorry
Onegaishimasu – would you like to practise with me?

The Japanese have two systems for counting. Here is one of them:

ich – one	kyu – nine
ni – two	ju – 10
san – three	niju – 20
shi – four	san-ju – 30
go – five	hyaku – 100
roku – six	sen – 1000
shichi – seven	ichiman – 10,000
hachi – eight	niman – 20,000

SOME JAPANESE CUSTOMS

When you go into a Japanese house, you take your shoes off and put on sandals.

● Japanese drink green tea. It is called ocha.
● Japanese like eating raw fish and special rice balls.
● Japanese take a lot of care over presentation. If they give a present, it is always very beautifully wrapped.
● Japanese spend a lot of time sitting on the floor.
● Japanese like hot baths. First of all they wash themselves thoroughly in a shower. When they are very clean, they sit together in one big hot bath.
● Japanese also drink a rice-wine called sake.

Japanese have a polite way of speaking to people. If they talk to Neil Adams, they call him Adams-san, which means Mr Adams. Sometimes they may call him Neil-san. But very few Japanese will call him Neil.

It is exactly the same with women. They will call Karen Briggs, Briggs-san. Sometimes they may call her Karen-san. But very few Japanese will call her Karen.

San is used for both Miss and Mrs.

Japanese sumo wrestlers are the biggest wrestlers in the world. Some weigh over 225 kilograms. The heaviest judo competitors rarely weigh more than 150 kilograms.

Japanese judoka never fight Japanese sumo wrestlers, because one wears clothes and the other doesn't. So no one knows who would win.

One of the religions in Japan is Zen, a kind of Buddhism. There are many interesting Zen stories. Here is one of them:

There was a Zen meditation teacher called Bankei.

He became so popular that all the people in the town stopped going to the other temple, and the priest from that temple got very annoyed.

He stalked angrily up to Bankei. He wanted to start an argument which he intended to win and get all the people back to his temple.

The priest said rudely: "Hey, Zen teacher! I don't respect you because you can't make me do anything."

Bankei answered: "Come here and I'll show you."

The priest pushed past all the other people and went to Bankei, eager to start the argument.

Bankei said: "Please, sit down on my left side."

The priest moved over to the left.

Just as the priest was about to sit down, Bankei said: "No, we will be able to talk more easily if you sit on my right side. Please, sit on my right."

The priest moved over.

Bankei said: "There you are. You are doing what I asked you to do. You are behaving perfectly well. Now, please sit down and listen like everybody else."

The Japanese Junior High School Championships – the competitors line up behind the flag banners of their schools in The Budokan, the most important judo competition hall in Japan

WRITING JAPANESE

In Japanese there are three different alphabets:

1 Kanji, the original Chinese characters
2 Hiragana, the method for writing Japanese words –
a bit like Japanese short-hand.
3 Katakana, a script for writing Western words.

Here is an example of kanji:

柔 **jū**

道 **dō**

技 **waza**

It sounds like this: judo waza. It means: judo techniques.

Here is an example of hiragana:

じゅうどう　が　すきです
jū　**dō**　**ga**　**su ki de su**

It sounds like this: Judo ga suki desu. It means: I like judo.

Here is an example of katakana:

バッキンガム　パレス

It means: Buckingham Palace.

This is your chance to write some Japanese. This is JUDO in kanji:
This is how you write it:

jū

dō

Most boys and girls in Japan can write about 1,000 different characters by the time they are 13. They can also write in hiragana and katakana, and many of them will know the European alphabet too.